CHAPTER LEADERS' HANDBOOK

Tactical Civics™ Field Handbook

Volume 1

TACTICAL ⬥ CIVICS™
Chapter Leaders' Handbook
Field Handbook Volume 1

MATTHEW S. MIDA

Co-Founder and IT Director, TACTICAL CIVICS™

Dedication

To all those who are "taking up the chores again".
May our efforts in Christ today restore
America's light of liberty and hope
for all generations to come.

CONTENTS

FOREWORD

When Matt Mida joined this mission over a decade ago, Americans were still in shock over 9/11 a decade earlier. Bush II was putting Big Brother in place so quickly, Americans couldn't react. Demonically clever, color-coded 'Terror Threat Level' warnings every few days traumatized the people as DC cynically "waged War on Terror".

Few Americans saw that DC was the terrorist, programming Americans as Communism has always done. Raise the specter of many invisible enemies, then convince the people that only government can save them. Liberals exposed the Bush/Cheney program for industry and Big Brother but conservatives refused to see until a decade later that the Bush family mafia were pals with the Clinton and Obama mafias; all part of one big DC Uniparty. After Bush II, eight years of Communism and racial incitement by a lifelong Marxist Muslim from Chicago. More than Clinton and Bush II, Hussein Obama gave globalists the keys to our republic, playing the race card daily to re-open old wounds.

Would this hijacking never end? When did it begin? Was there any way for We The People to arrest it? Matt came on board in 2010. With my brother Oscar and I, we dug into the origins and methods of the hijacking. There, in the annals and books of history, civics, and law, we discovered the players and mechanisms of *a hijacking that began in Lincoln's administration, in the shock and awe of the most destructive war in our history*. And this is the hardest truth for newcomers to accept. Obama, Biden, and the donkeys are only finishing what Lincoln and the elephants started for bankers and industrialists.

When Trump, the New York City developer and casino owner, became our best president in generations, millions looked to him as their savior. But he pushed the COVID fraud, reminding us of the Bush II tactic, and *no president has the authority and duties that belong only to the People*.

By God's grace, this handbook series will show you those duties and teach you how to do them. America need not be lost; repentance is always an option. And repentance is an *action* word.

D.M. Zuniga
New Bag End
Boerne, Texas

1

CHAPTER 1
Your Civic Duty

In the beginning of a change the patriot is a scarce man, and brave, and hated and scorned. When his cause succeeds, the timid join him, for then it costs nothing to be a patriot. — Mark Twain (1904)

America is collapsing quickly, and the reality is that no one officing out of DC has or ever will fix this situation; not the president, nor congress, nor the supreme court. Over the last 160 years we've allowed the federal creatures we created via the Constitution (legislative, executive and judicial) to give *themselves* powers that *we* never gave them. Having done that, by definition, is violating our highest law. Therefore, every single one of them is complicit in a massive criminal enterprise run from that 10 miles square city state on the Potomac.

Given that DC is full of criminals, would you expect them to police and limit themselves? Of course not! Would our Founding Fathers be intelligent enough to have created the greatest government that the world has ever known, yet not think this situation would ever arise? Is there a fatal flaw in their design? Of course not! They assumed that overreach by our federal servant would be arrested by 'We The People' who created that federal servant in the first place, using the enforcement institutions already in place at that time: *Grand Jury and Militia.*

Collectively, we have the responsibility and duty to enforce the law. The problem is, government schools long ago stopped teaching accurate American civics. So for five generations since Lincoln's war created a full-time paid army in direct violation of the Constitution, the people have been ignorant of our duties over our law. The legal industry tried to entirely erase the people's Grand Jury, while 'law enforcement' careerists and bureaucrats with the help of corporate media and with no help from frustrated private 'militia' groups, made the very word *militia* conjure up 'anti-government' rebels in the woods.

3

With We The People not watching the hen house, the foxes whose offices we created have been wreaking havoc. That must now change, or we will lose our unique Republic forever. If you choose to become a leader in your TACTICAL CIVICS™ county chapter, you will recruit, train, support, and organize 'We The People' in your county to *enforce* the Constitution for the first time in history! Yes, it's a new undertaking, but we promise it will be the most rewarding thing you have ever done in your life, and the TACTICAL CIVICS™ headquarters team will provide you everything you need to be successful.

If you wonder what success will look like: every county in America will have at least one TACTICAL CIVICS™ chapter (one for every 50,000 people). Each chapter's mission will be to superintend the congressman serving your district, to ensure that they obey the *Law* (Constitution). Your congressman will be just down the street working full time in his home district, so it will be easy to find out what (s)he is working on.

TACTICAL CIVICS™ will make it easier for county chapters, with the Indictment Engine™ app alerting the members automatically when their member of congress files legislation that is unlawful. All chapters will work together to ensure that Congress will forevermore operate under the strict limitations that we stipulate in the Constitution, instead of hiding out in DC, colluding with industry lawyers and special interests to do their bidding and build their fortunes. Monitoring our servants in congress will be as common as a farmer tending to his livestock every day. This oversight will be our daily civic chores, and we'll benefit from this perpetual vigilance in many ways. Americans will once again benefit from the fruits of their own labor, and communities will take care of each other as we did before beaureacrats conned us into believing they could handle our family's needs and hardships better.

For vision to become reality, two patriots in each county in America need to stand up and forge this new way of life with us. America is not a huge machine that we can 'fix' in one centralized change. We can only beat the huge monster in bite-sized pieces, thinking *locally* again. America is the sum of our 3,141 counties; with two dedicated members launching this new way of life in each county, we'll begin to turn the tide of history.

As a leader of this mission in your county, you will do more to preserve, protect and defend the Constitution than 100,000 U.S. troops overseas.

CHAPTER 2

Why Tactical Civics™ is Unique

Never before have we had a system to enforce the U.S. Constitution when it is blatantly disregarded. TACTICAL CIVICS™ has created the first framework for *constitutional law enforcement.* Having an active chapter of our private member organization in every county will be unlike any organization before. You must understand *how* and *why* we are unique so that as leaders of your county chapter, you will keep your chapter actions and goals aligned with those of TACTICAL CIVICS™.

First and foremost, AmericanAgain! Trust and its action mission TACTICAL CIVICS™ are proudly Christian. Our civilization has been collapsing because we allowed leftists and Communists to control the narrative, convincing Americans that there is no real truth; no good and evil. Whatever you feel like doing, 'just do it', as the shoe manufacturer boldly proclaims. They reprogram young Americans that no differences exist between men and women; you can choose to be either one! They teach that animals are more important than humans, and blacks far more important than whites. Paul teaches in Romans 1 that these are telltale signs of God's judgment on those who refuse to glorify Him.

TACTICAL CIVICS™ knows and teaches that truth does in fact exist, and is set out in Scipture. Our Christian faith informs and guides our values and actions as it did the Founding Fathers when they created our Constitution.

You do not have to be Christian to be a member. We accepts all legal American citizens and religions in America; even atheists. The only exception is followers of Mohammed. Islam is a cult, in a declared war against all non-Muslims. It imposes its own system of government and law on its followers, diametrically opposed to America's rule of law. Its avowed ultimate goal is to destroy American government and law.

TACTICAL CIVICS™ is also different from any other 'action' group in that, while we are involved in monitoring politicians, we never become involved in political candidates or electoral politics. We are an apolitical organization. Our purpose is to ensure that our elected servants adhere to the stipulated boundaries we set for them in the Constitution, to which they all take an oath to obey. Non-partisan, we do not electioneer for our members who run for office, and we define patriotism as: *We The People, making our servant government obey the U.S. Constitution.*

So we are true patriots; Americans focused on constitutional law enforcement to ensure our servants in government obey the law. Two critical aspects of constitutional law enforcement that set us apart from any other organization are restoring and coordinating the use of constitutional county Militia and Grand Jury. TACTICAL CIVICS™ county chapters will not officially participate in either group but no other organization in America is restoring or coordinating these two original law enforcement institutions stipulated in our Constitution, to keep our servants in line. We will discuss both institutions in the next chapter.

Finally, while TACTICAL CIVICS™ county chapters will educate the community in civics, we are not a 'civic organization' in the traditional sense. Our chapters will not engage in community assistance activities such as delivering meals, repairing homes for those in need, or adopting a local stretch of highway to clean up. Our mission is well-defined and laser-focused. Our mission objectives stipulated in the AmericaAgain! trust deed must not succumb to 'mission-creep' or we will not succeed.

CHAPTER 3

Critical Law Enforcement Components

Many organizations in America today see the corruption in our federal government; but only TACTICAL CIVICS™ has the full-spectrum solution necessary to restore our Republic because we are the only effort that has accurately isolated the real target: *organized crime.*

No amount of politics, whether passionate speeches and declarations, rallies and marches, or even elections can ever take the place of the law enforcement institutions that the framers of the Constitution inherited from their colonial ancestors, and from ancient England.

It is impossible to overstate the necessity for Grand Jury and Militia to restore and enforce our Constitution and the limited government it stipulates. Because so many state palaces are also in high rebellion against our supreme Law of the Land, TACTICAL CIVICS™ works with the county governments to restore constitutional Militia. And because Grand Jury is the first step to rooting out corruption at all levels of government, it also gives the County Militia its law enforcement aspect, and finally breaks through the deep divide between citizens and paid 'law enforcement'.

For much more on each of these vital action projects, read our **Field Handbook Volume 2,** *Grand Jury Awake*, a resource to educate members and your community about the history and your duty for Grand Jury, and our **Field Handbook Volume 3,** *American Militia 2.0™: An American Militiaman's Handbook*, for the constitutional and operational aspects of starting and running a Constitutional Militia.

Notice the diagram on the next page; it's a complete civics lesson in itself, illustrating the hierarchy of government as the Founding Fathers designed our Republic. Note the two enforcement elements: We The People, serving in our Grand Jury or Militia. Below that are our servant legislators. At the bottom are the federal bureaucrats, judges, and other servants.

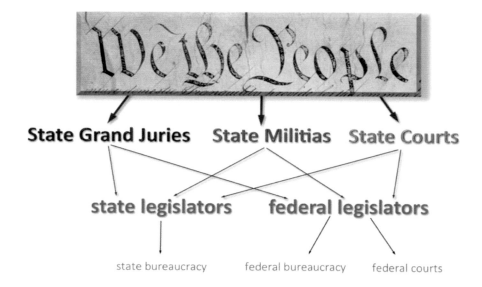

State Grand Juries   State Militias   State Courts

state legislators   federal legislators

state bureaucracy   federal bureaucracy   federal courts

The lesson of this diagram is that We The People have the ultimate duty to enforce the Constitution, using Grand Jury and Militia. All three branches government are corrupt; they will not arrest themselves! You and I and every patriot in America's 3,141 counties must step up and *do our duty*. Or as we say at TACTICAL CIVICS™, *do the chores*. So you need a basic understanding of the tools that the framers of the Constitution acknowledged, that America's first colonists had brought from England (600 years old at that time) for the People to deal with insurrection.

Stop Drinking That Stuff!

We cannot keep repeating pathetic tactics like emailing, letter-writing, holding protests like Venezuelans, on the steps of the grand palaces that we built for our servants, or waiting for the next election cycle to elect one more cup of fresh lemonade to pour into the 500-gallon vat of sewage that is official organized crime.

Your TACTICAL CIVICS™ chapter will educate the people of your county in the constitutional authority and role of Grand Jury and Militia, then restore both institutions so We The People can finally go to work arresting the criminals who flipped our government on its head.

8

The Grand Jury and Militia field handbooks are required reading for TACTICAL CIVICS™ County Chapter Leaders because it is vital to understand several things about the constitutional Militia and Grand Jury. Neither of these law enforcement institutions has exercised their original, ancient, lawful powers since Lincoln's war. There is widespread misunderstanding caused by deliberate misrepresentation by the legal industry, bureaucrats, and paid law enforcement defending their turf and their high positions of honor. As a result, We The People are living as ignorant victims...yet *we are actually the top level of government.*

TACTICAL CIVICS™ does not create or direct the Militia or Grand Jury. But we are the only organization educating Americans in how both institutions can and must work *together* to enforce our Constitution.

For Militia, our members need to identify people in the community who would be interested in forming a constitutional Militia. Once a group is formed, TACTICAL CIVICS™ county chapters assist the leadership of the Militia to get the county government to pass our model *Constitution Enforcement and Militia Ordinance.*

We Do Not Have to Take This

Grand Juries will convene in your county to investigate all potential serious (felony) crimes, whether being perpetrated by a city or county employee, whether in polling places, the DMV, mayor's office, county government, or even state or federal legislators whose offices and/or operations are in your county. This includes the recent, widespread overthrow of our government by stealing Election 2020. Once we finish ratifying Our First Right (see Appendix C) and get Congress to pass our proposed Bring Congress Home Act, we will have every legislator, state and federal, in our counties where a Grand Jury and Militia can enforce the law against their corruptions!

The Indictment Engine™ will provide initial evidence the Grand Jury can review regarding unlawful actions by the congressman from your district. If the Grand Jury believes there is sufficient evidence to indicate criminal activity, they will pass along the evidence to the county court for a formal trial.

Most Americans believe that the county judge is the only individual who can call for a Grand Jury. That is false. TACTICAL CIVICS™ county chapters will educate their community on how to bring public pressure to bear on judges and sheriffs to assure that a Grand Jury is impaneled whenever serious crimes are suspected in the county. It is crucial that the other institution of constitutional law enforcement, the Militia, is also restored, by county ordinance.

No, You're Not Going Crazy

For years, We The People (honest, productive Americans) have felt powerless and adrift in our own country. Our servants rule over us; with their black robes and their expensive suits, in opulent offices inside palaces that we paid for!

Something is very wrong with this picture. But until you learn civics, which American schools ceased teaching generations ago, our arrogant, corrupt servants will say they know better than you. They will claim to have authority over you that is nowhere in the Constitution.

That authority never existed. The People stopped allowing that kind of power even to their kings, *over a thousand years ago.*

We highly recommend that you download the *TACTICAL CIVICS™ Ready Constitution* in free PDF in the Training Center. Better yet, buy the spiral-bound, lay-flat edition. As you learn the Constitution, you will read right there in our highest law what the diagram on page 8 illustrates: We The People have always had authority to superintend our servants. We have complained and wasted our time and passion on electoral politics, *when we should have been doing law enforcement.*

Again, for further information on Grand Jury and constitutional Militia, read Volume 2 and Volume 3 of this Handbook, available in paperback at Amazon and as a free PDF online, in the TACTICAL CIVICS™ Training Center.

CHAPTER 4

Tactical Civics™ Training Center

The TACTICAL CIVICS™ Training Center (TCTC) is the central communication hub for all components of our mission. It is essential that you understand how it is organized, how to navigate it and how to use it to establish and maintain your county chapter. When doing any recruiting in person or online, you should point all potential members first to our TacticalCivics.com website. We designed that website to provide a quick overview of our mission and enough content to motivate people to create their free account in the TCTC to learn more.

A free membership on the TACTICAL CIVICS™ Training Center requires only name, email address, county, and state, and confirmation that you're an American citizen, and that you will respect our mission's Christian principles. With that information, you are given full access to the TCTC main network, a massive amount of educational content, and a complete explanation of our mission and projects.

As a potential leader for TACTICAL CIVICS™ it is imperative that you understand the intent and purpose of the Training Center. Every day we are inundated with examples of the criminal activities being perpetrated in DC. It has reached the point that it's all that everyone pays attention to and posts about in their social media accounts. This ensures that We The People will remain in a continuous state of agitation, fear and hopeless, leading to paralysis. Because such 'fear porn' does nothing to arrest the criminal actors or change our own attitude to take responsibility, TCTC moderators remove fear porn posts simply pointing out problems, and only allow content that furthers our mission.

Once a new member understands the mission and decides to take responsibility, they should subscribe to their county chapter. This allows a general member to become an official dues paying member in their county. In addition, it gives them access to their County Chapter private group.

Subscribing to their County Chapter group does not commit them to leading their chapter; it only gets the chapter on the map for TACTICAL CIVICS™ and allows others who join the County Chapter group to be immediately welcomed as we grow. Until a general member signs up for their County Chapter, they cannot participate in its activities.

To subscribe to your County Chapter, either type the name of your county and two letter state abbreviation into the 'Search TACTICAL CIVICS™ TRAINING CENTER field:

Or go to the Chapters section of the site and click on the 'Near You' button:

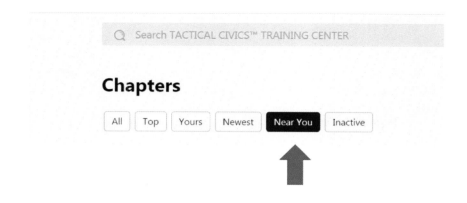

Once you see your County Chapter, click *Try Free*, then subscription, and enter your credit card information. Dues are $4.99 monthly.

As mentioned earlier, the TACTICAL CIVICS™ Training Center is the communication hub for all components of the mission, so as a potential leader of your County Chapter, you should become very familiar with it. The TCTC is broken up into two main networks: general membership network, and private County Chapter networks. Every member of the main network can see all posts and material in the main network. Any content posted in a County Chapter network is only visible to dues-paying members who have subscribed to that County Chapter.

The general membership network has four sections accessed from the 'Discovery' tab.

Welcome Section: New members should start here, and read these articles describing all components of our mission, and how to navigate the Training Center.

Topic Section: Currently there are 10 categories of topics; more will be added as needed. This section contains all the TACTICAL CIVICS™ materials available to members. *You must scroll right to view the complete list.* Each topic is a folder containing all available content of the TACTICAL CIVICS™ mission on that topic.

- **New Member FAQ** – Answers for common questions
- **Learn American Civics** – Articles, podcasts and videos that teach basic civics necessary to understand, in order to restore our Republic
- **Learn Constitutional Militia** – Articles, documents, podcasts and videos on the basics and more advanced Militia principles
- **Videos** – Mission overview videos
- **Tactical Civics Books & Resources** – Free PDF versions of all our books (can be downloaded free)
- **Blogs** – Over a year's worth of articles on current topics
- **Weekly Podcasts** – Archive of our past Sunday night podcasts
- **Monthly Newsletter** – Copies of our monthly newsletter
- **Tactical Civics Memes** – Memes to spread the mission on social media platforms
- **Promoting TACTICAL CIVICS™** – Resources to promote the mission in and through your county chapter

Featured Section: Popular and important articles in the TCTC

Events Section: Details for upcoming TACTICAL CIVICS™ national events.

Those are the core TACTICAL CIVICS™ Training Center sections on the main network.

See Chapter 6, Running Your County Chapter, for our discussion of the private County Chapter pages and what you should consider posting there for your chapter.

Finally, besides the core components just covered, there is a 'main news feed' or 'discussion wall' which works very much like social media platforms in which you can post comments, images, and files. In the upper right of your screen, is the ceneral chat thread with the entire group. It's the little icon with two 'talk bubbles'.

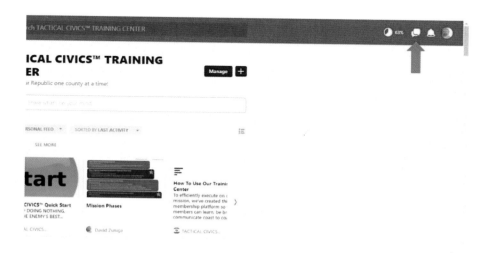

CHAPTER 5

County Chapter Leadership Team

TACTICAL CIVICS™ created, defined, and is leading a new way of life for productive, responsible Americans to restore our Republic. A new way of life unique to these united States, in which the People themselves oversee our public servants to ensure they obey our highest law, the U.S. Constitution, or face consequences. A key requirement for this new way of life will be to have an active, organized TACTICAL CIVICS™ County Chapter in every county in America. To ensure the County Chapters stay focused on the mission, two volunteer leaders (co-leaders) will be needed to run the chapter.

The two leaders for each county will take direction and guidance from your State Coordinator and the TACTICAL CIVICS™ Headquarters Team. As the mission is still in Phase 1 which includes planting a chapter in every county, we are still developing the framework for the county leaders. But here are a few of their responsibilities.

- Conduct monthly meetings
- Welcome new members to the chapter
- Listen to the Sunday Night national podcasts
- Actively participate in TACTICAL CIVICS™ Training Center
- Actively recruit new members in your county
- Be the first TC leadership point of contact for county members and refer all major issues to HQ
- Communicate w/State Coordinator to ensure state level mission work is accomplished successfully
- Educate the public on constitutional Militia and Grand Jury
- Schedule an annual TACTICAL CIVICS™ Gala to celebrate accomplishments, recognize affiliates, and welcome guests
- Partner w/nearby chapters as required to assist mission activities
- Lead your county chapter to complete all four mission phases

As TACTICAL CIVICS™ reaches national scale, responsibilities and roles may continue to be developed, refined, and communicated to all leaders. Our mission will not be easy, but it *will* be the most rewarding experience of our generation. Leaders must be flexible as we navigate this new way of life together. As a leader, you will have the full support of the Headquarters Team. If you need resources that are not available, we will do everything in our power to meet that need.

The purpose of having two co-leaders in each county chapter is so that responsibilities can be shared, and to ensure continuity of operations when a leader must step down short- or long-term, for any reason. TACTICAL CIVICS™ HQ leaves it up to each chapter to determine how responsibilities will be divided between leaders, as each situation is unique. There will be no other formal positions in the County Chapter besides these two leaders. First, because member groups tend to consume too much time and effort on useless 'politics'; secondly, because our mission is specific and focused. After all four phases of the mission are complete, ongoing activities – remember, just a responsible way of life – should be very manageable with limited leadership.

Initial term limits when a County Chapter is started will be four years for both leaders, but we encourage one leader cycling out after two years, allowing others in the community to take leadership and learn from the current leader. Thereafter, term limits are two years. Potential new leaders can self-nominate/volunteer or be elected by the membership.

Some necessary skills of the successful County Leader are:

- Good communication skills, written and verbal
- Level-headed personality; not easily angered/frustrated
- Computer skill (Word, Excel and PowerPoint or equivalents)
- A laptop or desktop at home is a plus (vs. only cell phone)
- Comfortable with public speaking; membership goal is half of 1% of the county population; a county of 50,000 will eventually have 250 members in the chapter
- Responsive. As a volunteer position, most will have full time jobs besides TACTICAL CIVICS™ but leaders must be able to respond to evening calls, texts and/or emails from chapter members, state, and HQ. This will require some time daily

Notice that I didn't say you have to be a constitutional scholar or have a PhD to qualify as a County Chapter Leader? We're looking for honest, hard-working Americans who care enough about the direction things are going, to work at shaping a responsible new way of life together for future generations to follow. We're the first in history!

If you're interested in applying for one of the leader slots in your county, send an email to LeaderInfo@TacitcalCivics.com and let us know of your interest. A member of the Headquarters Team will contact you to discuss next steps. To be eligible to apply, you must have filled out the Membership Info Survey online, and you must currently be subscribed to your County Chapter.

As membership grows, you will have opportunities to network with others in your county and adjacent legislative districts. Counties will organize events, as will state regions. Eventually, we will have statewide events varying from state to state by population and leadership teams. Regions will host their own meetings and events. We will be developing handbooks for higher leadership levels and events as we grow.

Remember: everything we do in this early stage will make a difference to future generations. We all feel extremely blessed and consider it a high honor to serve Christ and the Constitution in this mission. Every leader at every level serves at the pleasure of the TACTICAL CIVICS™ Headquarters Team and eventually of the nine-member AmericaAgain! Board of Trustees. Let's set a high standard for the future!

CHAPTER 6
Running Your County Chapter

Once you have at least one approved leader in your County Chapter, you can begin holding chapter meetings. As previously discussed, TACTICAL CIVICS™ HQ made a deliberate decision to keep chapter organizational process at a minimum. This allows leaders to focus on having the group learn the civics together, spreading the word about the mission, and executing on the action projects. We want to be 1000% more efficient than our servants in congress, though admittedly, that is not a very high bar!

The Chapter Charter

Chapter structure and operation should not be needlessly complicated. It should not be difficult to reach consensus on who should run meetings, keep notes, speak in public, or fetch pizza. If money is needed to print flyers, rent a hall, or buy pizza for a meeting or rally, take up a collection for the immediate need. Treasurers, bank accounts, State registration are unnecessary, and occasionally crippling complications.

TACTICAL CIVICS™ is the action mission to fulfill the purposes, and is bound by the terms, of the AmericaAgain! Declaration, which is available as an appendix to our spiral-bound *TACTICAL CIVICS™ Ready Constitution,* and in the Training Center. TACTICAL CIVICS™ county chapters are bound by, and limited to, the purposes in the Declaration and discussed throughout the Training Center and in our books. The County Chapter is to execute on the projects and purposes of TACTICAL CIVICS™ to the best of its abilities, and may use TACTICAL CIVICS™ intellectual property for those purposes, as directed by TACTICAL CIVICS™. Deviations from those purposes and direction will result in revocation of the charter and termination of those rights. A chapter is not a 'political action' organization for whatever a member may decide is a great idea.

Educating and organizing citizens for constitutional law enforcement action is the mission of TACTICAL CIVICS™. We do not do 'politics'; we educate Americans in their authority and duty to oversee their servant government as our Founders intended. We aid them to reassume our *collective* power and duty to enforce the limitations that We The People stipulate in our highest law. As opposed to partisan politics, we secure our own God-given rights by educating our neighbors to their duty and authority as Grand Jurors and as members of constitutional Militia.

A critical mass of citizens in every county must learn that Grand Jury has lawful power to investigate any wrongdoing, *especially* by public officers. When any Grand Jury impaneled has at least one member ready and able to educate the rest, corruption can be minimized in a county.

Militia is the only thing described as 'necessary' in our Constitution, so we seek to encourage existing Militia, encourage our community to form Militia if none exists, and educate Militia to its full constitutional duty and help it gain recognition by enactment of our model *Constitution Enforcement and Militia Ordinance.*

Frequent communication on the TCTC should be maintained with your State Coordinator and HQ Team, so that you stay aware of the latest teaching materials and policies. If you wish to make any customization of TACTICAL CIVICS™ materials, or create and distribute original materials, they must be approved by HQ before distribution. Keep records of chapter meetings and decisions, to avoid later confusion and because our activities are genuinely making history.

Seek members from all demographics and all walks of life. The essential qualifications are American citizenship, a love of and dedication to human freedom under God's Law, and commitment to restoring our constitutional system that was designed to secure them. Individuals with loyalties in conflict with these principles, including Muslims and members of secret societies such as Freemasons, are ineligible.

A membership oath to uphold the Constitution and all laws made in pursuance thereof, similar to that taken by public officials in your State, is encouraged. This will make clear to any who may be suspicious, the lawful nature of your chapter. Members should be strongly encouraged to pay dues to TACTICAL CIVICS™ by subscribing to your county chapter on the TACTICAL CIVICS™ Training Center site to support developing new materials and technical tools, and to staff the mission.

Leader Conduct

The initial two chapter co-leaders will be selected by self-nomination after the HQ Team has approved their applications. But the chapter should not insist on transferring leadership from a member who likes to hear his own voice or seeks power for its own sake. If any act or behavior taken by either leader in your chapter gravely violates the sentiment or normal accepted standards of behavior, we would expect the other leader of the chapter to swiftly deal with the situation in a manner appropriate to the act. If necessary, ask a member of the HQ Team to assist with any disciplinary action (also applies to the general members of the chapter).

Meeting Location & Format

As for location of the chapter meetings, there are many options. Meeting in a home or café when you are first starting out will be fine. As membership grows, look for a church, meeting room in your public library, VFW hall, or other such venue. Saturdays work best for most people. Choose a location fairly central in your county. If there is an owner of a restaurant, gun shop or other establishment in your county who is an outspoken patriot, try meeting there first; it's the most natural place to hold your meetings.

Choose a location that is not too loud. Set the first date and time and communicate it well in advance. Send reminders the afternoon prior.

The TACTICAL CIVICS™ Training Center has an events function for each county that can be used as the calendar for your chapter. It will send out reminders automatically.

Your meeting format and schedule can be at the members' preference; but you must give members a sense of usefulness, progress, and support. Monthly meetings are recommended, with tasks and milestones for members in between. Do not create needless procedural complication.

Do not allow your meetings to run long; respect potential new members' time. Your meetings should be sociable, but don't allow zealots to hijack meetings, veering from the mission into long discussions of partisan politics, eschatology, conspiracy theories, chemtrails, sports, or Trump diversions. *This is critical to mission focus.* We have specific milestones for each state. By laser-focusing on our targets, we *can* hit them.

Remember: this is not about 'being busy', but executing on specific objectives to restore this republic, county by county, one project and reform law at a time. We are all new to this; you or someone in your chapter may come up with an idea that changes American history, so always have your chapter send great ideas back up the chain to HQ.

At the end of each meeting, agree on a regular meeting time and place for next meeting. Meet at least once monthly, but your group may decide to meet weekly or biweekly if you wish.

County Chapter Webpage On TCTC

Between scheduled meetings, all county chapter members should be encouraged to continue learning the mission and civics, and interacting with other members across the county on the TACTICAL CIVICS™ Training Center (TCTC). In the TCTC, each County Chapter has their own private area that can be customized to fit their chapter's needs. Each person must subscribe to your County Chapter to gain access. This is also how dues are collected by the system. The County Chapter portion of the website has most of the main TCTC page's functions.

We give moderator access to the two co-leaders of the County Chapter, so they can modify and administer your county site. If a member of your chapter enjoys technical work, delegate the responsibility of updating the County Chapter site to that person.

Your county chapter website should be used for the following functions at a minimum:

- Use the 'Events' function to schedule your reoccurring chapter meetings. The system will keep track of RSVPs and reminders. It also allows you to integrate common virtual meeting systems such as GoToMeeting and Zoom.

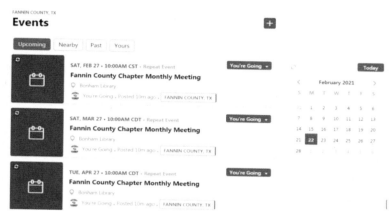

- Create Topics (folders) to organize local information, documents, meeting minutes, and the like.

- Use the all-county chapter member chat to communicate throughout the week with all members.

Member Maintenance

As a chapter leader, your County Chapter website also helps you maintain your membership roster. Any moderator of the group can download a membership list with useful information: name, email, date first joined, date last logged into the site. This lets you find inactive members, to follow up with them and encourage participation.

Annual Gala

One last county chapter activity for all chapters is an annual TACTICAL CIVICS™ Gala. Each year, the HQ team will determine a theme for the gala and communicate it to all chapters, providing all necessary printed and online visuals. Chapter Leaders will select a date and location, working with your members to plan food and beverages for the event. Besides your chapter members, invite all TACTICAL CIVICS™ Affiliates who have supported our mission during the year. Any chapter may decide to provide entertainment, invite the public, have an awards program to recognize members and affiliates who did outstanding work over the last year, or hold a donor-supported raffle of tactical gear to raise money for your chapter.

Summary

As TACTICAL CIVICS™ grows to scale nationally, we will further refine roles and responsibilities. The HQ team and State Coordinators will keep county leaders apprised of changes and will work with each chapter to make sure you are successful.

When you have questions, concerns or need assistance for the mission, just email LeaderInfo@TacticalCivics.com. In addition, every county chapter leader will be added to a private group at TCTC, to exchange ideas, ask questions, and get to know other leaders across America.

As a Chapter Leader you have the <u>authority</u> to:

• Lead your team

• Recruit, educate, and motivate others

As a Chapter Leader, you have the <u>responsibility</u> to:

• Build a chapter and keep it running

• Keep membership and project records for the chapter

• Promote TACTICAL CIVICS™ in public venues to educate citizens

• Participate in discussions, conferences and meetings

• Recruit new members, retain current members

• Raise funds for chapter activities

• Contribute ideas to improve our mission

As a Chapter Leader, you have <u>accountability</u> to:

• Regularly communicate with your State Coordinator and HQ

• Keep chapter records

CHAPTER 7
Community Engagement

County chapters will interact with the community in four ways: alliance with local Militia unit(s), community education events, TACTICAL CIVICS™ Affiliates, and TACTICAL CIVICS™ For Pastors.

Alliance With Area Militia

Obviously, we hope that every chapter will help the County Militia to be formed by enactment of the Militia Ordinance. But *your Chapter is not the Militia;* we're a private member organization. Militia is the public duty of all able-bodied citizens. Please see Volume 3 of the Field Handbook to learn about Militia stipulated by We The People in the U.S. Constitution.

Community Education Events

We recommend that once you know the material, you hold your local TACTICAL CIVICS™ Community Education kickoff event to introduce your county to the only full-spectrum solution to restore our Republic. Educating your community is critical to effective Grand Jury; half of our law enforcement action plan. This event will educate the community on our constitutional law enforcement and give your chapter greater visibility and credibility in your county.

To prepare for this important event, ensure the venue has the capacity to hold a large number of people; a church or auditorium is ideal. HQ will provide a video or PowerPoint presentation that can be displayed at the event so that our mission's message is consistent from county to county and state to state. Initially, it will be best to offer several such events per year until county residents truly understand the vital nature of constitutional enforcement via the Militia and Grand Jury, and so they are ready and able to fulfill their citizen duties when needed.

Civics *truly can be tactical,* when we return to the Founding Fathers' design.

TACTICAL CIVICS™ Affiliates

Perhaps your best friend owns a gun store. We can provide retailer kits for the firearms or tactical gear retailers, ranges, or training centers in your county who agree to support your chapter and who will sell TACTICAL CIVICS™ books, shirts, caps, stickers and other branded products. You remember the marketing line, *"The few. The Proud. The Marines."* Our mission will be 2000% more vital to American liberty than any military service. To re-train the American mind, we must build a 'cool' brand that becomes increasingly familiar to county residents.

Where possible, your chapter should work with gun dealers, tactical retailers, and feed or general stores to hold your meetings and events at their place of business. This generates traffic and interest in the retailer's establishment; in turn, the store becomes the area's headquarters of citizen action. *The Few. The Responsible. Tactical Civics™.*

TACTICAL CIVICS™ For Pastors

For too long, pastors have been encouraged to stay out of politics. By failing to address the real threats to our society, church attendance has dropped. Pastors are afraid to speak the truth! Ask any German how that abdication ends up.

Pastor, author, and radio host Mike Spaulding of Ohio has written *TACTICAL CIVICS™ For Pastors* to address this serious sin and to give pastors guidance and courage to lead the people to repent, stand up for Christ, and "do the chores" that the Founding Fathers assumed we would do.

APPENDIX A

Chapter Leader Agreement

1. As a Chapter Leader, recognizing that Tactical Civics™, a national member organization, seeks to grow and operate such that one or more chapters exist in every county in the contiguous United States, whose members are working for the same mission and objectives, and that Tactical Civics™ is organized in chapters to share best practices, I agree to keep my chapter focused on the organization's objectives, and not allow my chapter to involve itself in other projects or activities unless sanctioned in advance by headquarters.

2. I acknowledge that representing Tactical Civics™ is a privilege, not a right.

3. I agree to advance the mission of Tactical Civics™ by leading to the best of my ability with professionalism, perseverance, team spirit and my best ideas to promote this responsible way of life.

4. I acknowledge that perception is reality; that statements made or activities sponsored or performed by me or by members of my chapter that are antithetical to the AmericaAgain! Declaration or are otherwise morally or ethically questionable as compared to the traditional tenets of American Christianity, can be destructive to the TACTICAL CIVICS™ brand and morale of our membership. I agree to inform my chapter members of our policy: the first instance of any chapter member — including me — publishing, speaking or acting in such a manner as to bring TACTICAL CIVICS™ into disrepute will receive a warning. A second instance constitutes grounds for removal. On the third instance, the offender is expelled from our organization.

5. I agree to not use Tactical Civics™ business cards for personal or unrelated business.

6. I will do my best to spread the word about TACTICAL CIVICS™ online and in my county, especially with gun dealers and tactical retailers who show interest in hosting my chapter's meetings or events at their place of business to help such establishments become a hub of responsible citizen action in my county.

7. I agree to clear with headquarters any press release, other media piece, or community event or outreach project by our chapter and/or conducted in affiliation with any TACTICAL CIVICS™ Affiliate retailer before offering the story, event, or publication to the online or local community.

8. I agree that should I decide to no longer be involved with TACTICAL CIVICS™ for whatever reason, that I will not disparage the mission, its leadership, or the leaders or members of the chapter of which I will appear on record as Leader, nor will I use TACTICAL CIVICS™ materials, or represent its ideas as my own.

_____   _____

Signature of Chapter Leader   Date

APPENDIX B

Chapter Charter

Purpose

This Charter defines and describes a Chapter within the Tactical Civics organization.

The TACTICAL CIVICS™ organization exists for the purposes, and is bound by the terms, of the AmericaAgain! Declaration. As a part of TACTICAL CIVICS™, this Chapter is likewise bound, directed, and limited to those purposes.

This Charter confers upon this Chapter and its members the duty to advance the projects and purposes of TACTICAL CIVICS™ to the best of their abilities, and the right to use the intellectual property of TACTICAL CIVICS™ for those purposes, according the direction of TACTICAL CIVICS™. Deviations from those purposes and direction will result in revocation of this Charter and termination of those rights.

Name and Area of Operation

This Chapter shall be called [Your County Number X], and shall work in and recruit members from [Your County] or such smaller area as may constitute a district of approximately 50,000 people such as will comprise a Congressional district after the full ratification of Article the First from our original Bill of Rights.

This Chapter should also teach and recruit in surrounding areas with the goal of forming additional Chapters and should also be diligent to foster close cooperation and effective communication among nearby Chapters.

Tasks

Education is the mission and the tool of TACTICAL CIVICS™. We do not do 'politics'. We seek to educate Americans to their powers and duties of oversight of their servant government, so that We the People will supervise and operate that government as our Founders intended, and reassume our collective power and duty to enforce the law that defines and limits our government to its lawful purpose as securer of our God-given rights.

We seek to educate our neighbors to their duties and powers as Grand Jurors, and as members of Militia.

Enough people in every jurisdiction must know that Grand Jury has lawful power to investigate any wrongdoing including lawbreaking by officials, that any Grand Jury impaneled will contain at least one member ready and able to educate the rest.

Militia is the only thing described as 'necessary' in our Constitution, so we seek to encourage existing Militia, encourage our community to form Militia if none exists, and to educate Militia to its full constitutional duty and support it in seeking recognition through passage of our model *Constitution Enforcement and Militia Ordinance.* As a Chapter we also build local support for the national projects *Our First Right* and the *Bring Congress Home Act.*

Organization and Operation

Official structure and meeting format and schedule can be at the preference of the members; however, attention must be given to giving members a sense of usefulness, progress, and support. Monthly meetings are recommended, with tasks and milestones for members in between. Unnecessary procedural complication should not be created.

Frequent recourse should be made to TACTICAL CIVICS™ HQ to make sure you are aware of the latest teaching materials and policy decisions. Any customization of TACTICAL CIVICS™ materials you wish to make, or original materials you create and wish to distribute, must be approved by HQ before distribution.

Records should be made of Chapter meetings and decisions, to avoid later confusion and because our activity is making history.

Chapter structure and operation should be kept simple. It should be easy to reach consensus on who should run meetings, keep notes, speak in public, or fetch pizza. The group should not be afraid to insist on transferring leadership from a member who likes to hear his own voice or seeks power for its own sake. If money is needed to print flyers, rent a hall, or buy food for a meeting, take up a collection for the immediate need. Treasurers, bank accounts, and state registration are unnecessary and occasionally crippling complications.

Membership

Members should be sought from all demographics and walks of life. The essential qualifications are American citizenship, a love of and dedication to human freedom under God's Law, and commitment to restoring our constitutional system that was designed to secure them. Individuals with loyalties in conflict with these principles, including Muslims and members of secret societies like Freemasons are ineligible.

A membership oath to uphold the Constitution and all laws made in pursuance thereof, similar to that taken by public officials in your State is encouraged. This will make clear to any who may be suspicious, the lawful nature of your Chapter.

Members should be strongly encouraged to pay dues to TACTICAL CIVICS™ to support staffing our mission and continued, increased production of educational materials.

APPENDIX C

Our First Right

T his is the story of a crime. Of how a tiny mistake 140 years earlier set us up for it; of how We the People have always had the power to reverse it; and of how we can take Congress forever out of Washington DC, making that corrupt city irrelevant again.

America was hijacked by Washington DC, the most ruthless, powerful, criminal city-state in the history of the world, when Congress stole our First Right in the original Bill of Rights. This hidden mega-crime stole all representation in the U.S. House and Electoral College from residents of America's 31,000 small towns; over 90% of our land mass.

The millionaire lapdogs of billionaires and industry distract us with week-to-week nonsense as they fund pork, multibillion-dollar wars and multimillion dollar campaigns for huge districts with as many as 900,000 citizens. All because of a small error of just *one word*.

The Founding Fathers' Plan

On the last day of the five-month long Constitutional Convention in 1787, delegate Nathaniel Gorham made a motion to change one word in Article I of the proposed Constitution — *"the number of Representatives shall not exceed one for every forty thousand..."* to read, "for every **thirty thousand**". George Washington rose to speak for the first and only time to address the convention. On page 644 of *Records of the Federal Convention*, James Madison describes the scene:

> *"When the President rose...he said that although his situation had hitherto restrained him from offering his sentiments...he could not forbear expressing his wish that the alteration proposed might take place... The smallness of the proportion of Representatives had been considered by many members of the Convention an insufficient security for the rights and interests of the People. He acknowledged that it had always appeared to himself among the [disagreeable] parts of the plan...as late as the present moment was for admitting amendments, he thought this of so much consequence that it would give much satisfaction to see it adopted."*

It was adopted unanimously.

As state legislatures deliberated ratifying the Constitution, Madison's committee proposed 39 amendments. On September 25, 1789 Congress passed the 12-article Bill of Rights, sending it to the States to ratify. Article 1 guaranteed small districts…

Article the First. – After the First Enumeration required by the First Article of the Constitution, there shall be One Repre-sentative for <u>every Thirty Thousand</u>, until the Number shall amount to One Hundred; after which the Proportion shall be so regulated by Congress that there shall not be less than One Hundred Representatives, nor less than One Representative for <u>every Forty Thousand</u> Persons, until the number of Repre-sentatives shall amount to Two Hundred, after which the Proportion shall be so regulated by Congress that there shall not be less than Two Hundred Representatives, nor more than One Representative for <u>every Fifty Thousand</u> Persons.

Some people contend that *'not more than'* in the last sentence means they sought to *restrict* the number of representatives. But that word *'more'* in the last sentence was a transcribing error, as Washington's speech, the convention vote, and the bold clauses above demonstrate.

A Slip of Mister Otis' Pen

On the day before Congress officially passed the Bill of Rights, they agreed to correct a transcribing error to change the word *less* in *"the last line less one"* and to insert the word *more*. So the last sentence should end, "nor less than…":

Though confusing, the final phrase fits with the prior sentences. But the scribes making copies for the States received bad instructions from Samuel Otis, who reported that they should replace the word 'less' in the last *place* in the article, rather than in *'the last line less one'*. So the copies sent to the states contained an error that made the last passage read exactly *opposite* of what the Founding Fathers intended.

The handwritten copies were sent to all 13 states so that their state legislatures could ratify as stipulated in Article V. By 1790, twelve states had ratified: CT, KY, MD, NH, NJ, NY, NC, PA, RI, SC, VA and VT.

Our First Right...Hidden in the Basement

In 2011, a disbarred New Jersey attorney named Eugene LaVergne discovered that Connecticut's vote sat unrecorded, so only eleven votes were counted...all because of Mr. Otis' pen.

LaVergne discovered that the Connecticut House voted for the original First Amendment in October, 1789 and its senate voted for ratification in May, 1790. That made Connecticut the ninth state to vote for ratification out of 12 states at the time; exactly three-fourths of the states, the number required to ratify an amendment per Article V of the Constitution (now needs 38).

When its senate voted to ratify, the Connecticut House wanted to retract its earlier vote until Otis' error could be corrected. The transcription error was trivial; everyone knew the intention of that article was small districts. Since a ratification vote can't be retracted, Connecticut buried its ratification vote record in its state archives in the basement, and it was never recorded.

Although LaVergne sued in 2012, Article V does not give the courts jurisdiction in the matter. The only way forward is for the State legislatures to finish the ratification process.

Congress already passed it, so we don't need a constitutional convention; just 27 more ratification votes. DC can't keep 27 more State legislatures from restoring our First Right at last. But you may wonder, why did we wait so long?

Our 'Greatest President' Was Our Hijacker

In Essay 34 of our book, A Republic to Save, you will find links to six books and a website demonstrating that Lincoln and Marx were mutual admirers, and that Lincoln was the original hijacker of our Constitution.

Try to imagine your reaction if in just four years, *7.5 million Americans were to kill one another and destroy 50% of all property in America*. Adjusted for population growth, that's the shock-and-awe that Lincoln dealt us on behalf of his elite handlers, who have also controlled every subsequent president.

Once you grasp the existential shock to citizens, you can better understand why Americans did nothing even as DC organized crime went public with Lincoln and has grown worse ever since. For instance, given Americans' fear of their new master, Lincoln and the 37th Congress had no trouble hatching a counterfeiting operation.

We The People stipulate in the Constitution that only gold and silver are lawful U.S. money – but the chaos of his war gave Lincoln cover to create worthless paper 'greenbacks'. During 12 years of so-called 'Reconstruction', the U.S. supreme Court joined in the crimes of Lincoln and Congress as their co-conspirator with its Legal Tender opinions. No more checks and balances; all three branches are conspirators in ongoing felonies.

Congress' Crime of '29

The founders designed the People's House to keep politicians from amassing power. The number of districts of the House of Representatives was supposed to increase after every census to keep districts small. But the shock-and-awe of Lincoln's War and 'Reconstruction' were a devastating 16-year distraction. Elite puppeteers bought politicians, increasing their power and riches as their districts grew. Then, their only job was to distract America with weekly political scandals, which they do.

Congress reapportioned districts in 1872 with a random formula creating *292* districts, yet our First Right required *765* districts at that point. In 1890, the House changed its calculation to ensure that no state lost a seat due to shifts in population, yet our First Right required *1,844* districts as of the 1910 census, when Congress fixed the U.S. House at a random *435* districts!

Our First Right required *2,120* districts as of the 1920 census, but using convoluted math, Congress passed its Reapportionment Act of 1929, that did not even mention districts. When they used the excuse that the House chamber could not accommodate more than 435, congressman Ralph Lozier said:

> *I am unalterably opposed to limiting the membership of the House to the arbitrary number of 435... There is absolutely no reason, philosophy, or common sense in arbitrarily fixing the membership of the House at 435...*

Openly violating the Constitution, Congress arbitrarily fixed the size of the House, knowing that the original First Amendment was still before the States, open for ratification. Career politicians wanted power, and their billionaire handlers wanted it even more. Now we know *precisely* how it was done.

It's <u>Our</u> Responsibility

Isn't it amazing? This hijacking began with a one-word clerical error, followed by a shock-and-awe war and counterfeiting operation by the president that most American schools teach was one of our greatest.

We have an historic opportunity. The Internet is shaking humanity as the printing press shook the medieval world. We The People can arrest DC and end the hijacking. Reclaiming our First Right and restoring the People's House is up to We The People, the top level of government.

Eleven states already ratified, but at 39 state capitols, we must build Capitol Action Teams to push through the vote to ratify *Our First Right*. (First, we're growing TACTICAL CIVICS™ chapters for the even larger threat: the overthrow of our government in Election 2020.)

There is Precedent

The original Second Amendment was ratified by one man, after more than two centuries sitting idle in the states.

In 1983, a University of Texas student named Greg Watson began working to get 29 more State legislatures to ratify the amendment, which stipulates that if Congress gives itself a pay raise it does not take effect until an election intervenes. After ten years nagging the state legislatures, in 1992 that one young man got it ratified, and it became the 27th Amendment.

If one diligent citizen can do this, we can get 27 more state legislatures to ratify our First Right, the 28th Amendment!

Non-Partisan

George Washington's promised small districts are supported equally by the Left and Right. It is not a partisan issue, but a duty of *all* Americans to assure proper representation.

State Legislators

Remember, this is merely a state legislature *ratification vote, not legislation.* Yes, we must still deal with the long, drawn out calendar and rules and other nonsense in state legislatures. But the vote can be taken in one day; no legislation, reconciliation bill, or governor's signature required. TACTICAL CIVICS™ has PDF copies of our 28th Amendment Fact Sheet for Legislators, and draft Joint Resolution to call for the vote.

Granite Dome Syndrome

We The People must never trust a legislator. As an architectural engineer having designed buildings for almost 30 years, I'm well aware of the power of architecture on the human psyche. Ancient Rome employed that power to cause great conquered chieftains and princes to cower in awe when they visited Rome, the seat of their new master's power. *Granite Dome Syndrome* hits within a week of taking office...

You pay for it, so look carefully. Imagine that this instant opulence became *your* playground for life; like a middle-class person being given a free mansion with staff and amenities. The architecture alone makes the person consider himself very special. Of course, the staff reinforces this self-assessment every day. No legislator in a fancy capitol building is ever to be trusted. Politicians learn to think: *"The people pay all my bills…the fools even come hat-in-hand to my door every day. They pose for pictures with me! They send their children by the busload to get a glimpse of me! They call me Honorable! This is better than being a drug lord; I'm a rock star and my constituents are idiots!"*

As their sovereigns, we must put our foot down as our ancestors failed to do. That's what it will take to turn America around; stop expecting criminals to reform themselves. Why is the Internet not being used for self-government, as citizens on the Left and Right become daily more aware of the corruption in government, industry and professions? We *must* restore Our First Right, and put potential criminals on probation until further notice. We The People, on offense, cameras running.

The Bring Congress Home Act

Since 6,400 members will definitely not fit in the House chamber, we bring them home. Modeled roughly on the MOBILE Act of 2013, TACTICAL CIVICS™ is proposing reform legislation called the Bring Congress Home Act. It stipulates:

- No member of Congress can have an office in D.C.

- Every member gets one modest lease office, *in their town*

- Congressmen get 50% of their present salary

- Congressmen get a staff of two (senators, six)

- All members are limited to two terms

- All benefits end immediately

- They work via telepresence, off-the-shelf tech today

In each congressman's office space there will be one extra telepresence workstation for citizen use when we testify before a congressional committee or subcommittee. Why should *we* have to take time off, fly to them in DC, and pay for travel just to have them look down their noses at us, *their sovereigns?*

43

A New Chapter in American History

Once we set the precedent by bringing Congress home to modest lease spaces and small staffs, Americans in every state capital will get other great ideas. Former gubernatorial candidate and businessman John Cox of California launched a state-level project to break up the state legislature and have them serve full-time from their hometowns.

It will take time to reclaim life in America from the Deep State and its puppeteers in industry. But Our First Right *can* help stop the Deep State and industries sparking wars, corrupting our money and plundering the world in our name.

What About The Expense?

Imagine an employer who let employees set their own salaries, benefits, fancy offices, working conditions, staffing levels, and opulent perks; a recipe for business failure!

Americans complain about government excess, but still send the kids on DC bus tours to gawk at 535 politicians who *each* spend an average *$11 million annually* on their operations; who *each* have as many as *eight* offices and staffs; whose Capitol Hill palace is more opulent than those of kings, popes, and emperors, with white-glove dining rooms, gold-plated china, limousines, spas, private jets and more…paid for by us, their sovereigns; $5.85 billion annually for Congress' operations.

We The People abdicated our sovereign roles. We allowed our corrupt servants to control every aspect of our lives, steal us blind, and tighten the chains more with each generation. We have allowed them to rack up $23 trillion in debt and $190 trillion in unfunded liabilities.

Will a larger Congress cost us more? No; a decentralized local Congress made of normal Americans *will cut tens of billions and possibly hundreds of billions* in federal expenditures, plus saving us over $800 million annually in Congress' office operations alone. As Melancton Smith said in the 1788 New York ratification debate:

"The man who would seriously object to this expense to secure his liberties, does not deserve to enjoy them. By increasing the number of representatives, we open a door for…the substantial yeomanry of our country, who, being possessed of the habits of economy, will be cautious of…expenditures…a greater saving will be made of public money than [needed] to support them."

Think of this: for every *one-tenth of one percent* Congress cuts federal spending, they will again offset the entire cost of operations for 6,400 congressmen and 100 senators!

The Best Time in American History

The great deal of politically-generated anger and resentment in America today exists by design. Nothing serves Washington DC better than the American People at war against one another. This distracts us from the multi-billion-dollar crimes they are perpetrating in clear violation of the Constitution, right under our noses.

After the government overthrow of November 2020, the sky is the limit for Communists in Beijing and DC, now working together. And tens of millions more illegal aliens will soon be headed here…to vote!

Had enough? Take responsibility, and join TACTICAL CIVICS™. If you are a resident of KY, MD, NH, NJ, NY, NC, PA, RI, SC, VA or VT, your legislature already ratified Our First Right, but our mission is about much more than Our First Right, and we can do nothing until a critical mass of American get serious about our responsibilities.

Since winning our War for Indepedence, We The People have not had such opportunity to improve our own lives. Let's get to work!

— David M. Zuniga

About the Author

Matthew S. Mida was raised in rural West Texas on a small homestead where his parents taught him the value of hard work and honest living. His family and faith helped instill in him a sense of service to others that has guided him throughout life.

After graduating from Angelo State University with a BS in Biology and Chemistry, Matthew began his professional career as a public school teacher and taught for two years before transitioning to the IT field. For the past 22 years, Matthew has advanced up the corporate management ladder at major corporations including PepsiCo and JCPenney.

A lifelong Presbyterian, Matthew has always enjoyed studying God's word. An ordained elder in the Presbyterian Church, he has used his God-given talents in teaching adult and youth programs for most of his life. In the last year, he and his family were able to move full-time to his off-grid homestead in far north Texas where they enjoy raising livestock and being closer to God's creation.

Matthew and his wife Cheyenne have a beautiful blended family with three boys and one girl ranging from 13 to 19. Matthew's love for his children and concern for their future led him to join the AmericaAgain! mission in 2010.

At a time when most Americans are worried about the future of this Republic, Matthew's spririts are high and he is confident that the AmericaAgain! Trust and its TACTICAL CIVICS™ action mission can and will restore our Republic.

Made in the USA
Middletown, DE
09 October 2021

49864964R00033